Monday morning®

SUPER CIRCLE TIME
SPRING

by Patty Claycomb

Publisher: Roberta Suid

Production: Little Acorn & Associates, Inc.

SUPER CIRCLE TIME SPRING
Entire contents copyright © 2004
by Monday Morning Books, Inc.

For a complete catalog, write to the address below:
Monday Morning Books, Inc.
PO Box 1134
Inverness, CA 94937

Call our toll-free number: 1-800-255-6049
E-mail us at: MMBooks@aol.com
Visit our Web site:
http://www.mondaymorningbooks.com

ISBN 1-57612-202-6

Printed in the United States of America
9 8 7 6 5 4 3 2 1

Contents

Introduction

Spring has sprung! Spring is a season that pops up, grows, sprouts, and blooms. Spring is a great time to learn about how plants grow, the beauty of flowers, and the new magnificent look of leafy trees. Stand under a tree and look up. What do you see? You might see a bird nest, a canopy of leaves, or even strange looking seed pods. And don't forget the trunk! Look closely at it with a magnifying glass. Share your discoveries.

Spring is also a time for birth. Why do you think animals have babies in the spring? Can you imagine baby bunnies crawling out of a rabbit hole and hopping around in a foot of snow? Spring can stimulate creative discussions about warm weather, growth, the abundance of food, and animal habitats. Begin your discussion on your back, on a blanket of soft grass!

Spring is: Green–Growing–Flowers–Insects–Buzzing–Chirping–Umbrellas–Boots!

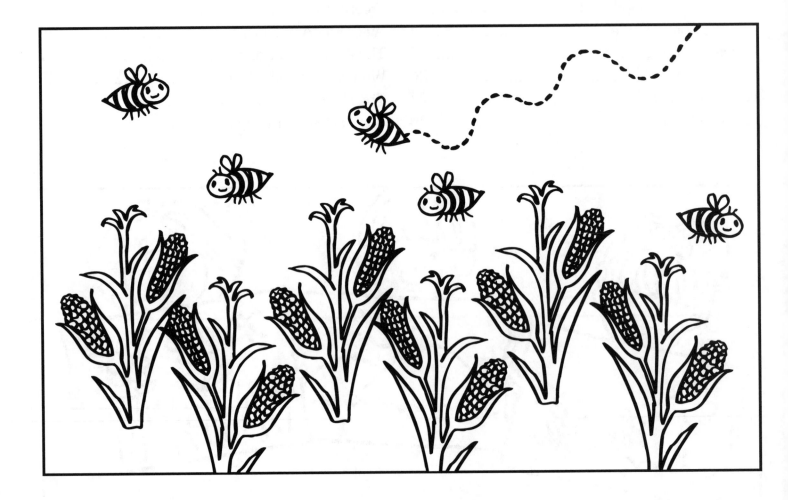

Green Spring

Things to talk about:

1. Ask the question: "Why do you think that many plants grow in the spring?" Brainstorm! The weather is warmer. Plants like the sunshine. Plants drop their seeds. More plants begin to grow.
2. Why do people say that spring is green? Possible answers might be: Plants and trees are green; Bushes are green; Leaves are green; Hills become covered in green grass; Plant growth produces the color green on the Earth.
3. In the spring, can you think of other things you might see that are green? Answers might be: green frogs, green caterpillars, green grasshoppers, green lily pads, green moss, and green weeds.

Materials:
Butcher paper, scissors, tape, a variety of green crayons

Preparation:
Cut a sheet of butcher paper. Tape it low on a wall.

Things to do:

1. Make a Green Spring Mural. Place different shades of green crayons on the rug.
2. Choose two or three children at a time to pick a crayon and draw something on the mural that is green.
3. Remind everyone of the green things you have talked about.
4. When your mural is finished, sit in front of it. Observe all the green things you have drawn.
5. Now say to the children: "There is something missing. It is something that helps everything grow green. What is it?" The answer is: The sun!
6. Draw a large circle near the top of the mural. Children can take turns coloring in the sun.

More Ideas:
• Go on a Green Spring Walk. Then talk about the green things you saw.

Springtime Chant

Things to talk about:

1. Ask the question: "If you were camping, and it was very cold, would it be a good idea to build a campfire?" Why? Brainstorm! The fire will warm the air around it. If you stand near the fire, you will feel the warm air.
2. What if you backed away from the fire. What would you feel? The cold air.
3. The air is warmer, in the spring, for the same reason. The sun is like a giant fire. If the Earth is closer to the sun, would you feel warmer or colder? Warmer.
4. During the spring, the Earth is closer to the sun. Clap if you like warm weather.

Materials: None

Preparation: None

Things to do:

Learn the *Springtime Chant*. Sing it to the tune of *The Worms Crawl In; The Worms Crawl Out!*

For the first line: Place fingers together to form a circle (the sun).

For the second line: From the sun shape, move hands outward.

For the third line: Place fingers and thumbs together on both hands to make leaf shapes. Then move hands slowly back and forth.

For the fourth line: Wiggle first fingers in the air.

For the fifth line: Cup hands together for a nest shape.

For the sixth line: Push arms straight up in the air, palms up! When you say the word "corn," raise your voice up.

For the seventh and eighth lines: Slowly move arms down and place them in a rocking position. Then rock them back and forth.

Springtime Chant

The days are warmer,
The nights are longer,
The trees have leaves,
And bumblebees!
The birds have babies,
And up comes corn,
To celebrate,
That life is born.

More Ideas:

• Practice this song as a fun memory game. Say each line, but leave out the last word. See who can remember what it is!

The Sunny-Side Up game

Things to talk about:

1. Who likes warm weather? Why? Can you do more things in warm weather, or cold weather?
2. Who has felt the warmth of the sun? How did it make you feel? Do you like feeling warm or cold? Why?
3. What are some different ways that the sun makes people feel? Brainstorm! Possible answers might be: hot, tired, lazy, happy, calm, peaceful, sweaty, and even wonderful.
4. Imagine what it would be like without the sun. What would happen?

Materials:

Yellow poster board, scissors, a black marker

Preparation:

Cut the poster board into card-sized squares. Draw a large circle in the middle of each card. Then draw a happy face inside two of the circles. Continue to draw a variety of matching faces inside the circles. Make at least one match for each child. Suggested faces are: happy, sad, dreamy, sleepy, scared, mad, and silly. The silly card can have three eyes.

Things to do:

1. Play the Sunny-Side Up Game. Shuffle the cards. Place them sunny-side down on the rug, in rows.
2. The child on your left can start the game. This child can turn over three cards. If a match is made, the child can take the two cards that match. If a match is not made, turn over all three cards.
3. When a card is turned over, identify the face. You might say: "It's the silly sun!"
4. If you have a large group, children can turn over four or five cards at a time.
5. Continue to give each child a turn to make a sunny-side up match.

More Ideas:

- Everyone can take their matches home in a plastic baggie. Add a few more sun cards that do not have faces. The children can draw their own matches at home.

Spring is Yellow!

Things to do:

1. Hold up a yellow sheet of paper. Ask the following questions: "What color is this?" "Why would the color yellow remind people of spring?" Brainstorm! Yellow is a warm color. It is the color of the sun. It reminds people of warmth.

2. What else is the color yellow? Answers might be: yellow butterflies, dandelions, roses, daisies, yellow apples, bananas, corn, parakeets, canaries, baby chicks, and baby ducks.

3. Look at each other's clothes. Who is wearing the color yellow? Can you think of something yellow that is in your house?

Materials:

Yellow construction paper, scissors, a felt marker

Preparation: None

Things to do:

Say the "Yellow Chant." As you say the first two lines, clap. When you say the word yellow, at the end of the second line, raise a fist high in the air.

When you say the third and fourth lines: Clap again. When you say the fifth line: Make a fist. Rotate it around and around in the air.

When you say the last two lines: Clap again. Raise a fist in the air as you say the word "yellow."

More Ideas:

- See who is wearing a spring color. Look for pastel colors.
- Go outside and look for spring colors.

Yellow Chant

Let's yell, let's yell,
Yell for the color yellow!
Yellow spring,
With a little green,
Mixed in with everything!
Let's yell, let's yell,
Yell for the color yellow!

The Spring Has Sprung Game

Things to talk about:

1. Say the sentence: "Spring has sprung!" Then ask the question: "What do you think that means?" Brainstorm!

2. During the spring, many things grow from seeds. Why do we plant seeds under the ground, instead of on top of the ground? Possible answers might be: A seed on the ground might get eaten by a bird; Seeds on the ground can get washed away by rain or stepped on; The dirt protects the seed.

3. If you were a seed, would you rather be a flower seed, an apple seed, or a pumpkin seed? Why?

Materials: None

Preparation: None

Things to do:

1. Play The Spring Has Sprung Game. Sit in a circle. Pretend you are tiger lily seeds. Dim the lights. Sit very still. You are resting under the earth.

2. The teacher can now say the "Seed Poem." Say it slowly. As you say the first and second lines: Place your hands on your head. Slowly weave back and forth. As you say the third and fourth lines: Place your palms together. Slowly move them upwards. As you say the word, "grow," wiggle your fingers.

3. The teacher can now say, "Roll up!" The children roll up into tight balls.

4. Now the teacher says: "Spring up!" Everyone can pop up and grow.

Seed Poem

I am under the soft brown earth.
I am moving so very slow,
Inching my way to the top of the ground,
Where you can see me grow.

More Ideas:

• Pretend to be snapdragons. Pop up and snap your fingers.

Circle Time—Spring • ©2004 Monday Morning Books, Inc.

Things to talk about:

1. Ask the question: "When I say the word *spring*, what do you think about?" Possible answers might be: warm air, rainbows, baby animals, insects, flowers, green grass, blue skies, tadpoles.
2. What do you think you might see on a warm spring day? A ladybug in the grass? People on a picnic?
3. If you could do one thing on a warm spring day, what would it be? Go swimming? How about resting in a hammock?

Materials:

Butcher paper, a marker, tape, scissors

Preparation:

Cut a strip of white paper. Tape it on a wall. Print the word "spring" on the paper.

Things to do:

1. Observe the word "spring." Count how many letters are in the word. Then say each letter.
2. Say the "Spring Chant" to the children. As you say it, point to each letter on the paper strip.
3. Say the chant again. Instead of pointing to the letters, do hand movements. Suggested movements are:

   For the two S lines: Make a circle with both arms.

   For the two P lines: Bend arms at the elbows and wiggle fingers for plants.

   For the two R lines: Hold hands downward and wiggle fingers for roots.

   For the two I lines: Touch your chest with both hands. Then make a fist and twirl it below your mouth for an eating motion.

   For the two N lines: Stick out both first fingers. Move them up and down and forward to represent swimming newts.

   For the G line: Clap.

   For the last line: Shake a fist high in the air.

Spring Chant

S - is the sun,
So big and round,
P - are the plants,
That grow all around.
R - is for roots,
That grow underground!
I - is for me,
Who likes to eat beans,
N - are for newts,
Who swims in streams,
G - is for green,
Green Spring!

More Ideas:
• Repeat the chant. Leave out the last word in each line. See if the children can remember what the word is.

Spring Artists

Things to talk about:

1. Ask the question: "What does an artist do?" Possible answers are: An artist can paint, draw, make statues, design buildings, design clothes, and create anything that the artist calls "artwork."

2. What does a landscape artist paint? This artist paints pictures of the outside. Name things outside that the landscape artist might paint. Answers might be: trees, mountains, lakes, flowers, meadows, clouds, and the ocean.

3. If you were a landscape artist, what would you like to paint?

Materials:

White construction paper, butcher paper, a variety of paint, brushes

Preparation:

Tape a large sheet of butcher paper on a table. Squeeze different colors of paint down the middle of the paper. Place sheets of paper around the table, with a paintbrush on each paper.

Things to do:

1. Pretend you are landscape artists. Take a walk outside. Observe the landscape. Comment on trees, the ground, the sky, flowers, weeds, curves in the land, mounds, holes, and anything that you might see.

2. When you have finished your walk, go back inside. Sit at the paint table. Paint what you have just seen.

3. When the pictures have dried, tape them on a wall. Label the wall: Art Show Now Open! Featuring exciting new landscape artists.

More Ideas:

Tape a long sheet of butcher paper on a wall. The children can take turns painting something that they saw on their walk. Place a sign by the painting that says "Landscape Mural." When it dries, have children print their signatures on the painting.

Things to talk about:

1. Ask the following questions: "Who likes to sing?" "Why do you like to sing?"
2. What parts of your body do you use when you sing? Possible answers might be: mouth, tongue, lips, voice, ears and even arms and hands.
3. What kind of songs do you like the best? Answers might be: silly songs, scary songs, songs about animals, songs you can dance to, western songs, or lullabies.
4. Sit quietly. Think of a song that you know. Can you hear it in your head? Would anyone like to sing the song that they are thinking about?

Materials:

A basket, paper, scissors, a marker

Preparation:

Cut paper into strips. Make a paper strip for each child. Print the name of a song on each strip. Place the strips in the basket.

Things to do:

1. Sit in a circle. Place the basket in front of you. Explain that it is a Song Basket. It is full of songs about spring and animals and insects.
2. Choose a child to pick a song from the basket. Read the name of the song. Sing it.
3. Add songs to your Song Basket as you learn new ones.

Note: Suggestions for songs and finger plays are on the next page.

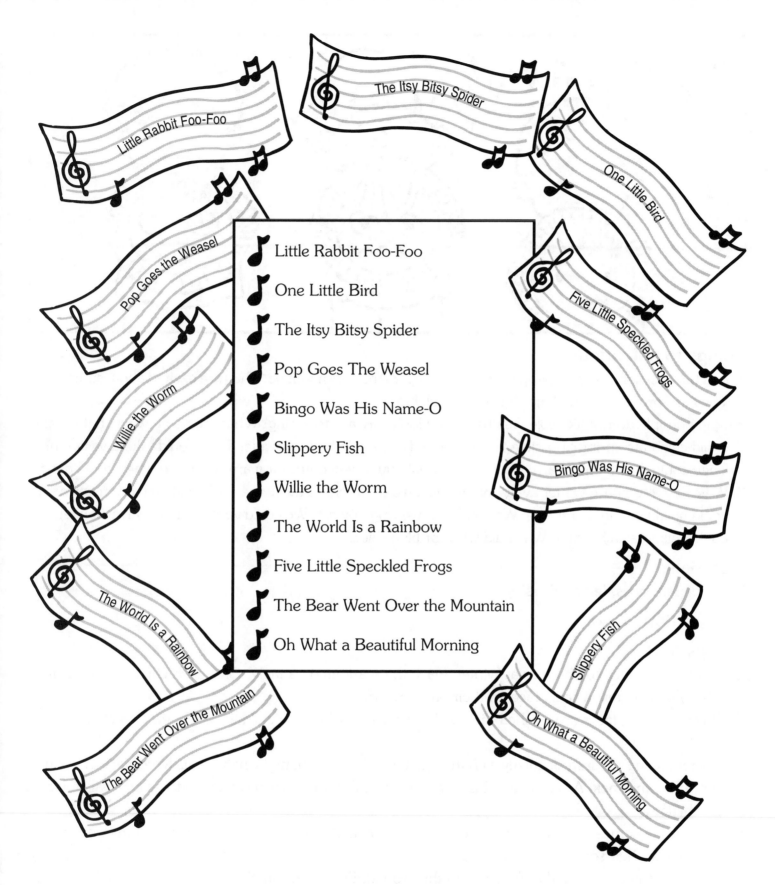

Little Rabbit Foo-Foo

One Little Bird

The Itsy Bitsy Spider

Pop Goes The Weasel

Bingo Was His Name-O

Slippery Fish

Willie the Worm

The World Is a Rainbow

Five Little Speckled Frogs

The Bear Went Over the Mountain

Oh What a Beautiful Morning

More Ideas:

• Have a wild card in the basket. It can have a special picture on it, for example, a rainbow. When this card is picked, the child can suggest a song to sing.

Chase It Away!

Things to talk about:

1. Ask the question: Why do people celebrate things? Answers might be: They are excited about something; They are proud of something; It is fun to celebrate.

2. Many people do not like cold weather. They look forward to spring. What are some ways that people could celebrate spring? Possible answers are: They could have a picnic; They could take a vacation; They could take a long warm walk; They could buy a new outfit for warm weather; They could dance.

3. We could also chase winter away. What could we do to chase away the cold weather? Brainstorm! We could build a fire in a fireplace; We could plant spring flowers; We could wrap up in a warm blanket; We could yell go away winter. We could wish for blue skies.

Materials:

Large paper plates, felt markers

Preparation: None

Things to do:

1. Make a scary face to chase away winter. Place the markers on a table. Give each child a paper plate.

2. Everyone can draw a scary face on their paper plates.

3. When the scary faces are finished, sit together on a rug. Choose a child to be winter. This child hides in the classroom.

4. The remaining children sit quietly with their pictures. Quietly chant: Winter wants to come back. Winter wants to come back. As you chant this, over and over, the winter child can begin to quietly walk towards the children.

5. As winter becomes very close, the teacher can count softly to three. On the count of three, everyone can hold up their scary pictures and yell, Boo!

6. Winter is scared away and melts down to the ground. Everyone can clap.

7. Continue to choose children to play winter.

More Ideas:

• After chasing winter away, go outside and celebrate spring with a sun dance. Wrap yellow crepe paper around the children. Tuck it into their clothes. Play music. Dance in the warm sunlight.

  Circle Time—Spring • ©2004 Monday Morning Books, Inc.

Rainbow Surprise!

Things to talk about:

1. In the spring, the weather can change very quickly. You can have sudden showers followed by sunshine. What are sudden showers? Brainstorm! A sudden shower comes very quickly and leaves quickly. What brings a sudden shower? A strong wind.

2. When you have a sudden shower and then sunshine, something beautiful can form in the sky? What is it? Offer clues. It is a rainbow.

3. Ask the questions: "Who has seen a rainbow?" "Where was it?" "What shape was it?" "Did you see any colors in it?" "What colors did you see?"

4. When people see a rainbow, they often say - "Wow! There's a rainbow. Come look!" Why do you think people get excited when they see a rainbow?

Materials:

Bowl, food dye, butcher paper, tape, crayons

Preparation:

Prepare for each activity listed below.

Things to do:

1. Make a rainbow in a bowl. Fill a large mixing bowl or pan with water. Everyone can take turns dropping a different color food dye in the water. Don't stir. The colors will swirl around the water by themselves.

2. Tape a long sheet of butcher paper low on a wall. Place a variety of crayons on the rug. Everyone can draw rainbows on the paper.

3. Learn the following "Rainbow Chant." Clap as you say it. When you say the word, violet, raise a fist in the air.

Rainbow Chant

Rainbow, rainbow, over me,
Tell me what you want to be,
Red,
Orange,
Yellow,
Green,
Blue,
Indigo,
Violet!

More Ideas:

• This makes a great jump rope chant. As an option, have two children swing a long jump rope low to the ground. Children can take turns jumping over it, back and forth, as long as they can.

• Children can also pair up and sit facing each other. Establish a rhythm by clapping each others hands and then clapping your own hands. Then say the chant.

Rainbow Hunt

Things to talk about:

1. Ask the question: "What does the word 'hunt,' mean?" Give an example: I am going to hunt for my lost sock. Brainstorm possible definitions.
2. Use the word hunt, in a spring sentence. Mama birds hunt for a safe place to build a nest. Ask everyone to try think of a sentence that involves the word hunt.
3. Ask yes or no questions using the word "hunt." For example: Do you like to hunt for Easter eggs? Have you ever gone on a bug hunt? Have you ever misplaced your pajamas and had to hunt for them?
4. What was the last thing you hunted for?

Materials:

White paper, felt pens, tape, scissors

Preparation:

Draw a rainbow on a sheet of paper. Cut it out. Tape it somewhere in the classroom. You can tape it on a wall, on a chair, in a shelf, or even over a cubby.

Things to do:

1. Sit together in a circle. Ask the questions: "How do you feel when you see a rainbow?" "Do you shout: A rainbow?" "Are you excited to have everyone see it?" "Why should you look at a rainbow right away?" They fade.
2. Go on a rainbow hunt. Have everyone slowly walk around the classroom. When a child sees the rainbow, he or she can yell: A rainbow. A rainbow.
3. The remaining children can gather near the rainbow and clap.
4. Now everyone can sit back on the rug. The child, who found the rainbow, can hide the rainbow.
5. Continue to hunt for the rainbow. If you have a large group, and not everyone has had a turn hiding the rainbow, continue the next day. Your rainbow has faded for the day.

More Ideas:

• You can also make five rainbows, instead of one. Hide the five rainbows around the classroom.

Root Investigations

Things to talk about:

1. Name some things that grow out of the ground. Possible answers are: trees, plants, cactus, grass, flowers, fruits, vegetables, and grains. Name some different fruits and vegetables.

2. All of the things that you named have one thing in common. What is it? Brainstorm! They all have some kind of root system that let's them soak up water.

3. Bend one arm at the elbow. This is a tree. Now place your other hand under the elbow of the bent arm. Wiggle your fingers under your elbow. These are the tree roots. They grow under the tree. Now ask the question: "How do the tree roots get water?" Brainstorm!

4. What is something else that the roots do for the tree, besides feeding the tree water? The roots hold the tree firmly in the ground.

5. When you buy a Christmas tree, and place it in your house, why does it dry out? Even though you water it, there is no root system to feed the tree water. Why can't you plant it in your backyard? For the same reason.

Materials: None

Preparation: None

Things to do:

1. Go outside and look for trees that have a large root system. You can see them poking above the ground. Touch them. Stand on them. Observe how strong they are.

2. Give each child a plastic cup, half-filled with water. Carry your cups outside. Look for a tree that you want to water. Stand around the base of the tree. Pour your water around the bottom of the trunk. Try to sense how good the tree feels as it drinks in the water.

3. Look for other plant life that might have a root system. Pull up any weeds or wildflowers you might see. Look for any roots attached. If you pull up flowers, bring them back to the classroom and place them in water.

4. Lay on your stomachs, in a grassy area. Gently pull up some grass. Can you see any roots? Dig with your fingers under the grass. Investigate.

More Ideas:

• Take pictures of the different trees around your school. Place them on a poster board. Print this question above the board: What do all these trees have in common?

Beans n' Things

Things to talk about:

1. Ask the questions: "If you plant an apple seed, what will grow?" "If you plant a flower seed, what will grow?" "If you plant pumpkin seeds, what will grow?"
2. What helps a seed to grow? Answers might be: Rich fertile soil, water and plenty of sunshine.
3. What happens to a bean seed when it has been watered for a few days? Brainstorm! The seed swells up. Then its outer skin splits open. Out pops a root.
4. What do you think the root does? It grows downward into the soil. It soaks up water.
5. What grows upward from the seed? A shoot. It pushes its way up until it breaks through the ground. Eventually, beans will grow on the shoots, and you can eat them.
6. What grows down? (Roots) What grows up? (Shoots!)

Materials:

A large glass jar, a paper towel, bean seeds, water, a spoon

Preparation:

Soak a jar in warm water to remove any labels.

Things to do:

1. Roll a paper towel into a tube shape. Place the paper tube into the glass jar. Press the sides of the paper towel, against the jar, with a spoon.
2. Place bean seeds in the jar, between the paper and the jar.
3. Spoon water into the jar until the paper towel is wet.
4. Place the jar in a warm sunny place. Water it daily. Watch what happens.
5. You will see roots growing down and shoots growing up.
6. When your bean plant gets to be five or six inches high, you can plant it in a pot or outside in the soil
7. Eventually it will grow beans that you can eat.

More Ideas:

- Make individual bean jars for each child to take home. Collect baby food jars. Plant one bean in each jar.

Pop Goes The Snapdragon!

Things to talk about:

1. Why do you think people plant flowers? Brainstorm! Possible answers might be: They are pretty to look at; They make your yard attractive; They smell nice; They attract butterflies and hummingbirds; They can be cut and put into a vase; Some people use them to make necklaces or to wear in their hair.

2. Obtain a picture of snapdragons. Look on flower calendars, garden magazines or the Internet. Hide the picture in a bag. Now ask the question: "There are flowers called snapdragons. What do you think a snapdragon looks like?" Brainstorm!

3. People discover new types of flowers and give them names. If you found a new species of flower, what would you name it?

Materials: None

Preparation: None

Things to do:

1. Sit in a circle. Choose a child to be the snapdragon. This child crouches down in the middle of the circle.

2. Now sing the following song to the tune of *Pop Goes The Weasel*.

For the first line: Point a first finger and move it around and around in the air.
For the second line: Place palms together and against a cheek.
For the third line: make two fists and open your hands on the words "wake."
For the fourth line: Place palms upward and push up toward the ceiling.
For the fifth line: When you say the word, "Pop," the snapdragon can sit up and growl.

Snapdragon Song

Around the town and under the ground,
A flower seed is sleeping.
Wake up, wake up,
And push yourself up,
Pop goes the snapdragon!

3. The snapdragon can now choose another child to be the snapdragon. Continue until everyone has had a turn to be the snapdragon.

More Ideas:
- Plant an entire garden of snapdragons. Have everyone crouch down at the same time. The teacher can sing the song. When the teacher says the word, "Pop," everyone can sit up and Growl.
- Have a variety of flower names printed on strips of paper. Read them to the children. Each child can choose to be a different type of flower. For example: *Pop Goes the Pansy!*

The Blossoming Tree

Things to talk about:

1. Close your eyes. Picture a tree in your mind. Look at it for a few seconds. Now open your eyes. Have everyone describe to you what they saw.

2. There are many hidden things in trees. There are things that you only see if you look closely. Try to name some of them. Brainstorm! Possible answers are: Pine cones, seeds, nuts, blossoms, bird nests, birds, and ants crawling up the trunk.

3. In the spring, the first blossoms appear on a tree. What does a blossom turn into? A flower.

4. Why do you think trees begin to grow flowers in the spring? The weather is beginning warm up.

Materials:

Butcher paper, tape, scissors, crayons, a variety of colored bows

Preparation:

Cut a large sheet of butcher paper. Tape it low on a wall. Draw a large tree on the paper. The children can color in the tree.

Things to do:

1. Sit by the tree picture. Talk about the tree. Mention its trunk, leaves and roots. What does the tree need to grow healthy and strong?

2. Tell the children that something special is beginning to grow on the tree. Brainstorm!

3. Now have everyone close their eyes. While eyes are shut, stick a bow on the paper tree. Then have everyone open their eyes. What grew on the tree? A blossom.

4. Place the remainder of the bows on the rug. Each child, in turn, can choose a blossom and stick it on the tree.

5. When everyone has placed a blossom on the tree, observe how beautiful it looks.

6. Name the colors you see on the tree. Count the blossoms.

More Ideas:

• Make individual pictures of blossoming trees. Everyone can draw a tree on a sheet of paper. Then color your trees. Now pinch up small squares of white or colored tissue paper. Glue them on your trees.

Insects in Your Shower!

Things to talk about:

1. Ask the following questions: "What is another name for insect?" Bug. "Where can you find bugs?" Brainstorm! Everywhere. Name different places, such as, in your backyard; in the woods; in grass; under rocks; in your house and even in your shower.

2. What do all of us have in common? Answers might be: We all have two legs, two arms, a head, two eyes, a stomach and a heart. Name as many things as you can.

3. What do insects have in common? Answers might be: Insects have six legs. They have three body parts - the head, middle and bottom. Some insects have wings. Some insects have antennas. Some insects have no ears, but feel vibrations and movement. Some insects live in large colonies or cities.

4. Would you rather be a grasshopper, a bee or a butterfly? Why?

Materials: None

Preparation: None

Things to do:

1. Go outside and look for insects. Look for them under rocks, on leaves, on tree trucks, in the grass and in the air.

2. Go back inside and draw an insect that you saw. Use a variety of markers.

3. Pretend to be roly-polys. Lay flat on the rug. When you scare a roly-poly, it curls up into a ball. (The teacher can tap each child on the shoulder.) You are scared. Curl up in a ball.

4. Pretend to be grasshoppers. Stand in a grassy area. Keep your feet together. See how far you can jump.

5. Divide the children into two groups, the spiders and the butterflies. On the count of five, the spiders can chase the butterflies. If the butterflies are tagged, they sit on the grass and are caught in the spider's web. Play again. Have everyone change roles.

6. Build beetles. Have the children bring in shoe boxes. Add pipe cleaners, glitter, cotton balls, crepe paper and tissue paper for wings. Create your own bug.

More Ideas:

• Find round or oval shaped rocks. Paint them to look like ladybugs. Take your pet ladybug home.

Hide-a-Bug

Things to talk about:

1. Ask the question: "If you were a bug, how would it feel to be so tiny?" "Would it feel fun?" "Scary?" "How would a blade of grass look to you?"
2. Where would a good hiding place be, if you were a bug? Brainstorm!
3. Why would you spend part of your day hidden from view, instead of in plain sight? Answers might be: Birds might eat you; People can step on you; You might get run over by a bike or car; You might need protection from rain or wind.
4. Many bugs live under rocks. Do you think that is a good idea? Why? Why not?

Materials:

Smooth rocks, bug stickers

Preparation:

Collect smooth rocks, at least two for each child. You can find smooth rocks at pet stores, candle shops, floral shops or even beaches. Place a bug sticker on the bottom of each rock. Make sure there are matching pairs of stickers under the rocks.

Things to do:

1. Sit in a circle. Place the rocks, sticker-side down, on the rug.
2. Choose a child to be the bug hunter. This child carefully turns over two rocks. Turn slowly so you don't scare them away.
3. If a match is made, the child can take the two rocks. If there is not a match, the child turns the rocks back over, in their same place.
4. Continue until all the matches have been found.
5. Send each match home in a plastic baggie. Poke holes in each baggie so the bugs can breath.

More Ideas:

- Place only one of each match on the rug. Everyone, in turn, can turn over a rock. Each child keeps the rock he or she turns over. Then hide the remaining rocks. Everyone can hunt for the rock that matches the one they chose.
- Hide them inside or outside.

Where is Beetle?

Things to talk about:

1. What colors do insects come in? All colors. Name as many colors as you can.
2. What shapes do insects come in? Many shapes. Try to describe different kinds of insects, such as, a ladybug, a butterfly and a dragonfly.
3. Do you think insects talk to each other? Yes. Insects communicate when they live together in colonies. They interact through smell, taste, and touch.
4. If you couldn't use your voice to speak, how else could you communicate?

Materials: None

Preparation: None

Things to do:

Sing the song, *Where is Beetle?* Sing it to the tune of *Where is Thumbkin?*, using the same hand movements.

Where is Beetle?

Where is beetle?
Where is beetle?
Here I am,
Here I am,
How are you today sir,
Very well, I thank you,
Fly away,
Fly away.

Where is bumblebee?
Where is bumblebee?
Here I am,
Here I am,
How are you today sir,
Very well, I thank you,
Fly away,
Fly away.

Where is dragonfly?
Where is dragonfly?
Here I am,
Here I am,
How are you today sir,
Very well, I thank you,
Fly away,
Fly away.

Where is grasshopper?
Where is grasshopper?
Here I am,
Here I am,
How are you today sir,
Very well, I thank you,
Fly away,
Fly away.

Where is ladybug?
Where is ladybug?
Here I am,
Here I am,
How are you today sir,
Very well, I thank you,
Fly away,
Fly away.

More Ideas:
• Sing the song often. Think of different insects to use in the song.

Ladybug Grass

Things to talk about:

1. Ask the following riddle: "What is red, round, has black dots and can crawl up your arm?" (A ladybug.)
2. Ask the following questions: "What is a ladybug?" It is an insect. "How can you tell it's an insect?" It has six legs. "How many legs do you have?" "Are you an insect?" "What are you?"
3. Do ladybugs have wings? Yes. Why can't you see them when they are resting or crawling? Brainstorm! They tuck their wings under their hard red shell.
4. Where can you find ladybugs? Anywhere. Brainstorm different places, such as, trees, flowers, in the grass, on a rock, on a park bench, or even on you.

Materials:

Butcher paper, green crayons, tape, red markers and red crayons

Preparation:

Cut a large strip of butcher paper. Tape it low on a wall.

Things to do:

1. Sit by the butcher paper. Place green crayons on the rug. Choose a few children at a time to color tall blades of green grass on the paper.
2. When everyone has had a turn, sit back and observe your grass. How would you feel if you lived in that grass, as a tiny bug? Would you feel scared? Would it be fun?
3. Now ask the question: "What's missing?" Brainstorm! There are no insects in the grass!
4. Place red crayons or markers on the rug. Everyone, in turn, can draw a ladybug in the grass.
5. When everyone has drawn a ladybug, sit back and observe your ladybug grass. Ask questions, such as, "What do you think they are doing in the grass?" "How many do you see?" "What could scare them away?" "Is it okay to pick up a ladybug?"

More Ideas:

• Some ladybugs are yellow and green. Have the children draw yellow and green ladybugs in the grass, after they have drawn the red ones. Which ladybug is your favorite?

Poly-Poly Pound

Things to talk about:

1. Are most insects large or small? They are considered small creatures on the earth. Do you think it would be scary to be so small? Why?

2. Insects are small, but they can take care of themselves. It what ways can they protect or defend themselves? Possible answers are: They can fly away when danger approaches; Some insects bite; They can hide underneath things; Some smell bad, so no one will eat them; Some have hard shells that protect them; Some can camouflage themselves.

3. There is one very small insect called a roly-poly. If he is scared, what do you think he does? He rolls up into a tight ball. This protects the soft parts that are easily hurt.

4. Your soft parts would be your head and your stomach. Have everyone roll into a ball. Are your head and stomach protected?

Materials:

A small dark colored ball, such as, blue, black or purple

Preparation: None

Things to do:

1. Sit in a circle. Pretend the ball is a roly-poly. A large blackbird has frightened it.
2. Use the blackbird pattern on page 31 to make a headband from poster board.
3. Choose a child to wear the headband. This child sits in the middle of the circle.
4. Now sing the following song to the tune of *London Bridge*. Clap as you sing it.

Poly-Poly Round

Roll the roly-poly round,
Round and round,
Round and round,
Roll the roly-poly round,
Past the blackbird!

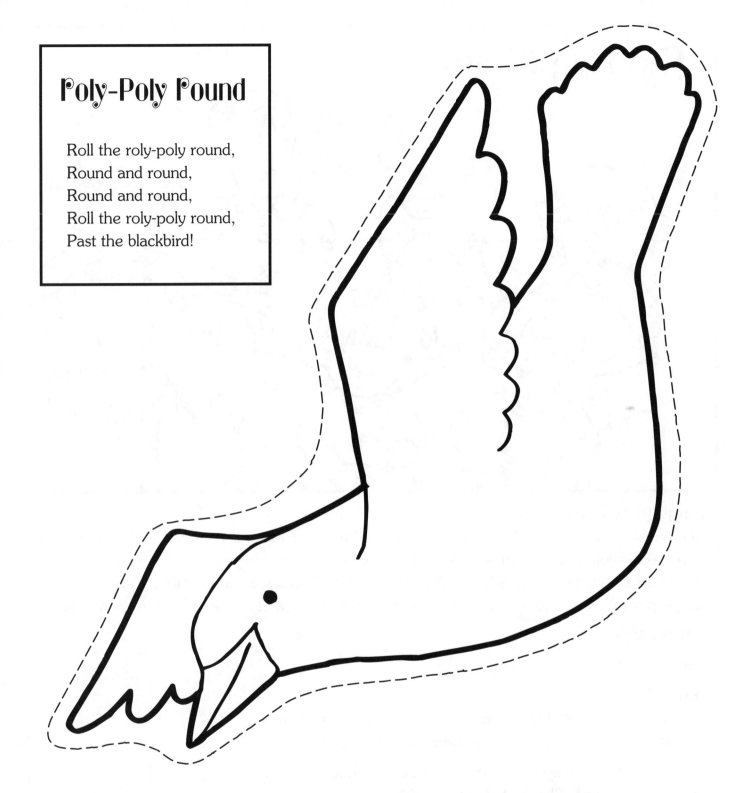

5. After you have finished the song, give the ball to the child on your left. This child tries to roll the roly-poly past the blackbird. The blackbird tries to grab the roly-poly before it reaches another child. If he does, both children switch places, and the song is sung again.

6. If the blackbird does not catch the roly-poly, he remains in the circle. Sing the song again. The child who caught the roly-poly, rolls it.

More Ideas:

• If you have many children, two blackbirds can sit in the circle.

The Bug Chant

Things to talk about:

1. It is hard to describe something in only one word. Ask everyone to describe a butterfly, using one word.
2. How would you describe yourself, using one word?
3. Name an insect, such as, a ladybug. Then have the children say what color they associate a ladybug with. Name more insects. Ask the children to name a color that relates to each insect.

Materials: None

Preparation: None

Things to do:

1. Say The Bug Chant. Talk about the word that follows each insect.
2. Below are suggestions for body movements.

   For the word run: Slap your thighs in a running motion.

   For the word swat: Clap both hands together.

   For the word splat: Slap one of your upper arms.

   For the word pat: Stick out a first finger. Pat it with your other hand.

   For the word jump: Slap both thighs once with both hands. Then bring hands up.

   For the word roll: Roll your fists around and around.

   For the word phew: Hold your nose and wave your remaining hand in the air.

   For the last line: Wag your finger.

Bee..........Run!
Fly..........Swat!
Mosquito..........Splat!
Caterpillar..........Pat!
Grasshopper..........Jump!
Roly-poly..........Roll!
Stink bug..........Phew!
Don't touch anymore!

More Ideas:

• Make up your own *Bug Chant*. Use insect names. Have the children think of the word that ends each line.

Honey Tummys

Things to talk about:

1. Ask the questions: "Who has tasted honey?" "Where did you get the honey from?" "Did the people at the market make the honey?"

2. Who makes honey? It is an insect. Brainstorm! It is the honeybee.

3. Have everyone show their tongue. What does your tongue do? It helps move your food around in your mouth, while you are chewing. A bee's tongue is much longer. It sips up nectar in flowers. This nectar is brought back to the hive and made into honey.

4. How do you think a bee brings back the honey? Does she carry it in a bucket? Brainstorm! She stores it in her honey tummy.

5. If you were a flower, and you wanted to attract a bee, what color would you be?

Materials:

Masking tape

Preparation: None

Things to do:

1. Explain that scout bees fly away from the hive and look for flowers. When they come back, they do a special dance. The movements, in the dance, tell the bees where the flowers are.

2. Using masking tape, stick the tape in a large figure eight pattern. When the flowers are far away, the bees dance this design.

3. Choose a child to be the bee dancer. This child can begin at a starting point. (Tape an X at one end of the figure eight loop.) The child can walk the pattern until she returns to the X. While she walks, everyone else can buzz.

4. Continue to choose children to dance the bee dance. As an option, play music.

More Ideas:

• Make two patterns, one a figure eight and the other a large circle shape. When the flowers are near, the bee dances in a circular design. Each child can choose their dance.

The Honey Bee Song

Things to talk about:

1. Ask the question: "If you see a bee, what are some things you could do?" Brainstorm! Answers might be: Leave him alone; Try to catch him with a net and observe him, then let him go; Run away; Follow him: Watch him.
2. What do you think would be the best thing to do? Stand very still. If you move quickly, you might scare him. What happens when you scare a bee? He gets scared. Then what does he do? He might sting you.
3. What do you do when you get scared?

Materials: None

Preparation: None

Things to do:

Sing this song to the tune of *The Itsy Bitsy Spider*. Sing it slowly and with suspense.

For the first line: Place the tips of your fingers together, in both hands. Wiggle them.
For the second line: Pinch first and second fingers together in one hand. (Buzz for about five seconds after you sing the line.)
For the third line: Point to each of your eyes.
For the fourth line: Bend arms at elbows, with palms together.
For the fifth and sixth line: Freeze!
For the seventh line: Place a hand over eyes in a "looking," position.
For the eighth line: Rub your tummy.

When you say the words, "freeze," sit still.
When you say "run,"
slap your hands on your thighs in a running motion.
When you say, "oh no," place each palm on each cheek.
When you say, "knee," point to your knee.
When you say, "ouch," slap your knee!

The Honey Bee Song

A little tiny honey bee,
Buzzed all over me. (Buzzzzzzzz)
Maybe he will see,
That I'm not a honey tree,
And if I do not move,
Perhaps he'll fly away,
And look for pretty flowers,
To sweeten up his day.

Freeze!
Run!
Freeze!
Run!

Freeze! Oh no!
He landed on my knee!
Ouch! He stung me!

More Ideas:

- Explain that different flowers make different types of honey. Taste some clover and orange honey. Can you taste a difference?

firefly flash

Things to talk about:

1. Ask the question: "What is a firefly?" An insect. What is special about a firefly? Offer a clue. It is also called a glow worm. It glows.

2. What part of a firefly's body glows? Guess until the correct answer is given. The firefly's abdomen glows. Accept stomach.

3. What do you think a firefly does with his glowing abdomen? Does he use it like a flashlight? Does it keep him warm? Brainstorm! The firefly flashed his glow to attract other fireflies. They also use it to communicate with.

4. What part of your body would you like to glow? Your ear? A hand? How about your hair?

Materials:

A flashlight

Preparation: None

Things to do:

1. Sit in a circle. Dim the lights. The teacher holds the flashlight. Pretend it is a firefly.

2. Sing the following song to the tune of: *Michael Row Your Boat Ashore*. As you softly sing it, pass the flashlight around the circle. Be careful with your firefly. He is delicate. Don't drop him.

Firefly, Firefly

Firefly, firefly,
In the night,
Firefly, firefly,
Glowing bright.

Firefly, firefly,
In the night,
With your light,
I can see,
Little stars,
In the tree.

More Ideas:

• Send a note home requesting a flashlight from each child. Sing the song with everyone
  holding a firefly. Swirl the lights around the classroom as you sing.

The Butterfly Story

Things to talk about:

1. What do you think is the most beautiful insect? Brainstorm! The butterfly is considered the most beautiful insect by many people. Why? Their wings have many beautiful color on them. Name colors. Each one you name is on a butterfly wing.

2. Ask the following questions: "What is a baby butterfly called?" A caterpillar. "Would somebody like to describe a caterpillar?" Answers might be: Long, soft, many legs, a big head, horns, stripes, and can be many colors.

3. Does a caterpillar look like a butterfly? No. How does a caterpillar change into a butterfly? Brainstorm! The caterpillar builds a cocoon or chrysalis. It stays inside the chrysalis for a week. It dissolves much of its body and grows new parts. It now has wings.

4. How does the butterfly break out of its chrysalis? Some butterflies gulp large amounts of air. It swells up and splits the chrysalis. Then it pushes itself out. Everyone can take a large gulp of air. Are your cheeks puffing out? Do you feel your chest expanding?

5. What does the butterfly do now? It flies away.

Materials:
A small clear plastic ball

Preparation: None

Things to do:

1. Place the ball on the rug. Sit around the ball. Tell "The Butterfly Story."

2. As you tell the story, act it out. When you finish the story, ask if anyone would like to try to tell "The Butterfly Story." Find suggested movements on page 40.

When you say egg, point to it.

When you say hatched, clap!

For the third, fourth, and fifth lines: wiggle a first finger.

For the sixth and seventh lines: open and close one hand, with thumb and fingers touching.

For the eighth line: place both first fingers together so tips touch.

For the ninth line: rotate fists around each other.

For the tenth line: pretend to sleep.

For the eleventh line: when you say pushed, ram a fist into an opened palm.

For the next three lines: flap your hands like wings.

For the last line: point to the egg.

The Butterfly Story

Once there was an egg.

It hatched!

Out came a caterpillar.

The caterpillar was hungry.

He ate leaves.

He ate and ate and ate and ate!

He ate until he grew bigger.

Then he spun himself a cocoon.

He rested inside the cocoon for a week.

After a week, he pushed himself out of the cocoon.

He now had wings.

He was a beautiful butterfly!

He then flew away.

Eventually, he laid an egg.

More Ideas:

• Print "The Butterfly Story." Tape it on a wall. The children can draw eggs and caterpillars and butterflies. Tape their drawings around the story.

Circle Time—Spring • ©2004 Monday Morning Books, Inc.

Big Eyes!

Things to talk about:

1. Ask the question: "There is something very large on an insect's head. What is it?" Brainstorm! His eyes.
2. Guess which insects have very large eyes. These insects are: Bees, flies, dragonflies, the praying mantis, and butterflies.
3. Why are many insect eyes so big? Answers: It is easier to find food with large eyes. Big eyes help them watch out for enemies that catch and eat them. Big eyes detect movement quicker. It is easier to get away.
4. Look at your face. Is there a part of your face that is very big? Are your ears bigger than your eyes? Is your nose bigger than your ears? Do you think you see or hear better?

Materials:

A chair, dragonfly and fly patterns, poster board

Preparation: Make two poster board headbands. Color, cut out, and attach a dragonfly to one and a fly to the other.

Things to do:

1. Sit in a circle. Choose a child to sit on a chair, in the middle of the circle. The child is the dragonfly.
2. The child can try and widen his or her eyes as big as possible, keeping the head forward.
3. Now choose a child to be the fly. This child can sit behind the chair and slowly crawl towards one of the sides.
4. The dragonfly waits until he or she sees movement off to one side. The fly can try to scare the dragonfly before he is noticed.
5. Once the fly has startled the dragonfly, choose two different children to play the roles of fly and dragonfly.

More Ideas:

- This can be played outside. Place chairs on a grassy area, in a row. If you have twelve children, use half the number. For example, you will place six chairs on the grass. Then choose half the children to be dragonflies. These children sit in the chairs. The remaining children are the flies. The flies can creep up on the dragonflies and try to scare them. Once scared, the dragonflies can fly away, with the flies chasing them. Then change roles

Spider Surprise

Things to talk about:

1. What is a spider? It is not an insect. An insect has six legs. It is an arachnid. An arachnid has eight legs. Say arachnid slowly. Clap each syllable.
2. What do spiders do every day? They spin webs. What is a web made of? It is made of silk. How do they make silk? It comes out of a body part called a spinneret. It is on their abdomen. Say spinneret slowly. As you say it, rotate your fists around each other.
3. What does a spider do after she spins a web? Brainstorm! She waits and waits and waits and waits. What is she waiting for? She is waiting for her meal.
4. What gets caught in a spider's web? Name a variety of insects.

Materials:
Yarn, scissors, tape, a toy spider

Preparation:
Cut a long string of yarn. Tape it between two heavy objects, above the ground.

Things to do:

1. Pretend the yarn is a string of silk spun by a spider. Choose a child to be the spider. This child holds the toy spider or a poster board spider (page 42).
2. Now choose a child to be the fly. This child can very quietly crawl towards the web.
3. When the fly reaches the web, he or she can slowly move the yarn up and down.
4. When the spider feels the vibration of the web, the spider can slowly creep towards the fly. The spider can tap the fly on the shoulder. Everyone can yell, "You're caught!"
5. Choose different children to be the spider and the fly.

More Ideas:

• Make a giant spider web. Take a skein of yarn and tape it back and forth, between and around furniture. Overlap and underlap. When you have finished, everyone can lay under the yarn web. Look up. How does it feel to be trapped in a web?

The Little Baby Spider

Things to talk about:

1. Ask the question: "Why do you think many people are afraid of spiders?" Brainstorm! Possible answers might be: They look scary; They can bite; Some are poisonous; They can jump on you.

2. Spiders do something really good for the earth. What do you think it is? Brainstorm! They eat many insects. Without spiders, there might be twice as many flies.

3. Some spiders build new webs every night. Can you imagine having to build a new house to live in, every single night? Why is this easier for a spider to do? He doesn't need furniture.

Materials:

A shoe box, white yarn, scissors, paper, a pen

Preparation:

Cut strings of yarn for spider webs. Cut many. Place them in a shoe box. Cut strips of paper. Reproduce and cut apart the different versions of the song, *The Itsy Bitsy Spider*, listed on page 45. Examples are listed below. Place the song strips in the shoe box. Mix them up with the yarn.

Things to do:

1. Place the "web" box on the rug. Sit around the box.

2. Choose a child to place their hand in the web box. The child finds a strip of paper and give it to the teacher.

3. The teacher then reads the name of the song. Everyone sings it. Each song will be sung to the tune of *The Itsy Bitsy Spider*. Substitute for *The Itsy Bitsy Spider* the words that are on the word strip.

4. Examples of the songs are listed below:

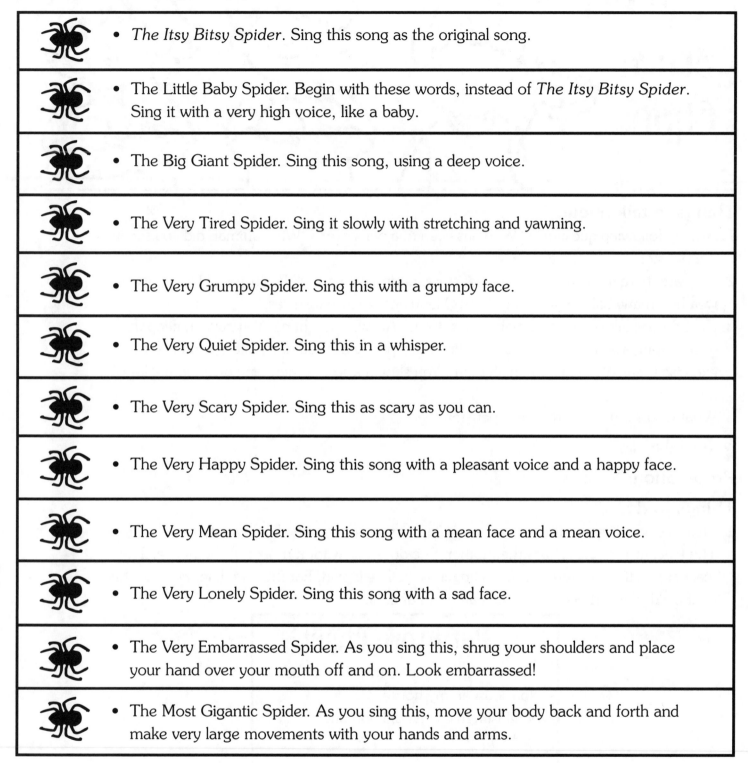

- *The Itsy Bitsy Spider*. Sing this song as the original song.

- The Little Baby Spider. Begin with these words, instead of *The Itsy Bitsy Spider*. Sing it with a very high voice, like a baby.

- The Big Giant Spider. Sing this song, using a deep voice.

- The Very Tired Spider. Sing it slowly with stretching and yawning.

- The Very Grumpy Spider. Sing this with a grumpy face.

- The Very Quiet Spider. Sing this in a whisper.

- The Very Scary Spider. Sing this as scary as you can.

- The Very Happy Spider. Sing this song with a pleasant voice and a happy face.

- The Very Mean Spider. Sing this song with a mean face and a mean voice.

- The Very Lonely Spider. Sing this song with a sad face.

- The Very Embarrassed Spider. As you sing this, shrug your shoulders and place your hand over your mouth off and on. Look embarrassed!

- The Most Gigantic Spider. As you sing this, move your body back and forth and make very large movements with your hands and arms.

More Ideas:

- Have everyone bring in a shoe box. Make web boxes to take home. The children can cut up strings of yarn to place in their box. Add paper spiders that the children can draw and cut out.

The Pet Store Chant

Things to talk about:

1. Ask the following questions: "Who has been to a pet store?" "What animals did you see in the pet store?"

2. Why are there many animals, in a pet store, during the spring? Brainstorm! During warm weather, many baby animals are born. Many end up in pet stores.

3. How do you take care of animals in pet stores? Answers might be: You have to keep their cages clean; You have to make sure they have plenty of food and water; You have to exercise them; You have to brush them; You should also pet them and give them a lot of attention.

4. What would a good name for a pet store be?

Materials: None

Preparation: None

Things to do:

1. Sit in a circle. Say the following chant. Clap as you say the first line. For the second line: The teacher pretends she is the mother. She does not want a mouse in the house. The teacher and the children can wag a finger as the line is said. For the third line: Point to the next child in the circle. This child names an animal.

Pet Store Chant

I went to the pet store to buy a mouse,
No mouse in my house.
So (Jasmyne), what did you buy?
(A dog)

---

2. Repeat the chant. Continue to ask the children to name different animals, each time you say it.

3. When everyone has named an animal, try to remember all the animals that were named.

More Ideas:

• Draw a large store shape on a sheet of butcher paper. Place markers on the rug. Everyone can draw an animal in the pet shop.

Feathered friends

Things to talk about:

1. Have everyone extend a first finger. Pretend there is a bird perched on it. Ask the question: "What does your bird look like?" Answers might include: It has a beak, two eyes, two wings, feathers, legs, feet, toes, a tail, and a specific color.

2. See who can finish this sentence: Birds are the only animals who have (what?) Feathers. What do feathers do? Brainstorm! They allow birds to fly. They keep them warm. They also keep them dry.

3. Do birds lay eggs? Yes. Where can you see bird eggs? In nests. What does a mother bird build her nest with? Answers might be: twigs, grass, mud, moss, roots, feathers, ribbons, strings, and even human hair.

4. Most birds sleep at night. There is one bird who spends the day sleeping and wakes up at night to hunt. What bird is this? An owl. Owls can sit motionless on a branch. They can be hard to see. Try to sit as still as you can.

Materials:
Yellow posterboard, a black marker, scissors

Preparation:
Reproduce a happy face card for each child.

Things to do:

1. Give each child a happy face card. Explain that the happy face stands for a "yes!" The teacher will make statements about the birds that have a yes or no answer. If you feel the answer is yes, you can hold up your happy face.

2. Below are suggested comments:

- Birds have feathers. (yes)
- Birds lay eggs. (yes)
- Birds have four wings.
- Birds fly by flapping their wings. (yes)
- A hummingbird is a large bird.
- Birds eat meat. (yes)
- Birds love to take baths. (yes)
- Birds cannot swim.
- The ostrich is the largest bird in the world. (yes)
- An ostrich can fly.
- Owls hunt at night. (yes)
- A mother bird keeps her eggs warm by sitting on them. (yes)
- Some birds have webbed feet. (yes)
- A baby swan is called a cygnet. (yes)
- Birds have very heavy bones.
- Woodpeckers make holes in trees for their nests. (yes)
- Penguins have feathers. (yes)
- An ostrich lays tiny eggs.
- When a baby duck hatches out of its egg, its feathers are dry.
- A roadrunner lives in the desert. (yes)
- If you see a bird egg, pick it up.

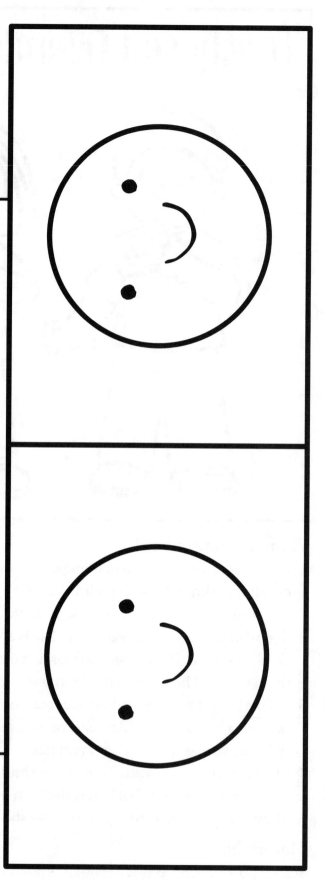

More Ideas:

- Make a copy of the comments for each child. Send them home with everyone. Ask parents to read the comments. Encourage the children to remember the answers.

Baby Bird, Baby Bird

Things to talk about:

1. Ask the question: "Where do all babies come from?" Brainstorm! They come from their mothers.

2. Do animal mothers take care of their babies? Most of them. What do they do? They clean their babies with their tongues. They give their babies milk. They bring their babies food to eat. They build safe places for their babies to grow.

3. How do baby ducks learn to swim? Their mother walks them into the water. The baby ducks follow her example. How do baby birds learn how to fly? The mother bird encourages them to use their wings when they are old enough to fly.

4. A mother pig is not a very attentive mother. Guess what she does after she has her babies? Brainstorm! Newborn piglets have to take care of themselves. Their mother does not clean them or help them to feed. They have to push and shove to drink her milk.

Materials: None

Preparation: None

Things to do:

1. Sit in a circle. Say the following chant to the rhythm of *Brown Bear, Brown Bear*. Each child can think of a different baby animal to name during the chant. The teacher can begin with baby bird.

2. Below is an example of the chant:

Baby Bird, Baby Bird

Baby bird, baby bird,
What do you see?
I see a baby cat,
Following me!

Baby cat, baby cat,
What do you see?
I see a baby mouse,
Following me!

Baby mouse, baby mouse,
What do you see?
I see a baby snake,
Following me!

Baby snake, baby snake,
What do you see?
I see a baby deer,
Following me!

Baby deer, baby deer,
What do you see?
I see a baby wolf,
Following me!

Baby wolf, baby wolf,
What do you see?
I see a baby bear,
Following me!

Baby bear, baby bear,
What do you see?
I see a baby girl,
Following me!

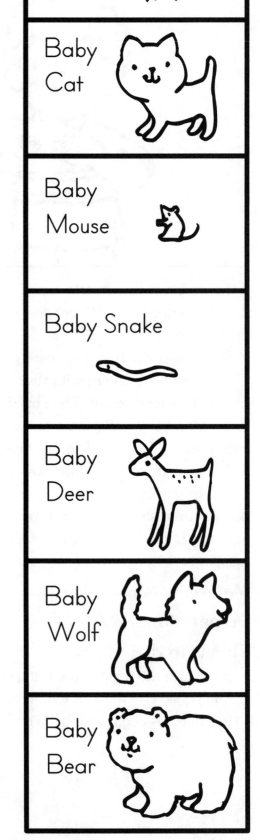

Baby Bird

Baby Cat

Baby Mouse

Baby Snake

Baby Deer

Baby Wolf

Baby Bear

More Ideas:

• Instead of every child thinking of an animal, give each child a
picture of an animal. Each child can say the animal name during
the chant. Then place the pictures on the rug. Everyone can pick
the animal they want to say in the chant.

Spring Babies

Things to talk about:

1. Ask the question: "Why do you think many animals have babies in the spring?" Brainstorm! Possible answers are: The weather is warmer; Babies would not survive well in cold weather; There is more grass and plants and food to eat on the ground; Baby animals have time to grow big and strong before cold weather comes.
2. Where are baby animals born? Possible answers are: Some are born in nests. Some are born underground in burrows, such as, rabbits and fox cubs. Some are born near ponds, like ducklings. Some are born in woods, like baby deer.
3. Who takes care of you after you are born? Who takes care of baby animals? Their mothers. What do their mothers do? They clean them. They feed them. They warn them if there is danger near.

Materials:
Blue butcher paper, or blue construction paper, masking tape, scissors

Preparation:
Cut a large sheet of butcher paper. Tape it on a rug area, away from the circle time area. This is your duck pond.

Things to do:

1. The teacher can pretend she or he is a mother duck. The children are the duck eggs. Have everyone curl up on the rug.
2. Dim the lights. It is dark inside an egg. Remain very quiet. When the teacher says, "pop," the children can hatch from their eggs.
3. As soon as ducklings hatch, they see their mother. They follow her everywhere. The teacher can walk around the classroom, with her ducklings following.
4. The teacher can eventually reach the pond. Baby ducks can swim right away. The ducklings can follow their mother duck into the water.
5. Swim around. When the mother duck senses danger, she quacks loudly. The baby ducks dive under the water.
6. When the mother duck feels it is time for her babies to rest, she can lead them back to their nest area. Everyone can huddle together and rest from their first outing.

More Ideas:
• The teacher can lead her baby ducks outside. Follow an obstacle course. Set one up or walk around play structures, underneath them, and on them.

Quack, Quack!

Things to talk about:

1. Ask the questions: "Who has a voice?" "Where does you voice come from?" Have everyone make a sound with their voice.

2. Did you make sounds as a baby? Did you all have the same cry, when you were babies? No. Everyone has a different sound to their voice. Even babies.

3. Do you think your mother recognized your cry? Yes. If she heard two babies crying, she would be able to tell which one was you. For example: If you were hungry, you might cry in short gasps. Another baby might cry in one long wail. Try to imitate both of these sounds.

4. Baby animals have their own sounds, also. A mother duck knows the sounds of her babies. What does a baby duck sound like? Try a duck sound. The sound comes from deep in their throat. They just open their beaks and it comes out. They don't have to form different sounds with their lips, like we do.

Materials: None

Preparation: None

Things to do:

Say the following chant to the tune of *Baby Sharks*. Say the first set of hyphenated words quickly. Pause at least one long second before you say the remaining two words that are similar.

For the first verse: Move your fingers and thumbs up and down in a talking motion. Move them along with your established rhythm.

For the second verse: Hold a fist in front of you for an egg. With your other hand, make a shh sound with your first finger against your lips.

For the third verse: Clap in rhythm.

For the fourth verse: Raise a fist in the air. Shake it to the rhythm.

For the fifth verse: Slap your thighs in rhythm, like you are waddling.

Baby ducks peep-peep, peep, peep,
Baby ducks peep-peep, peep, peep,
Baby ducks peep-peep, peep, peep,
Baby ducks peep-peep, peep, peep!

In an egg shh-shh, shh, shh,
In an egg shh-shh, shh, shh,
In an egg shh-shh, shh, shh,
In an egg shh-shh, shh, shh!

Time to hatch pop-pop, pop, pop,
Time to hatch pop-pop, pop, pop,
Time to hatch pop-pop, pop, pop,
Time to hatch pop-pop, pop, pop!

Here I am quack-quack, quack, quack,
Here I am quack-quack, quack, quack,
Here I am quack-quack, quack, quack,
Here I am quack-quack, quack, quack!

Off I go slap-slap, slap, slap,
Off I go slap-slap, slap, slap,
Off I go slap-slap, slap, slap,
Off I go slap-slap, slap, slap!

More Ideas:

• The children can take turns being the mama duck. Make a
mama duck and several baby duck headbands for children
to wear. The mama duck can lead her ducklings around the
classroom.

Freeze Bunny

Things to talk about:

1. Why do you think baby bunnies are often born in the spring? Brainstorm! It is warmer weather. Baby animals, like bunnies, need to be kept warm.
2. How do you think mother bunnies keep their babies warm? She pulls off large amounts of her hair. Then she covers her babies with it.
3. What do you think happens when baby bunnies begin to crawl? Brainstorm! They leave their nest. They twitch their noses to smell the air. They thump their hind feet when they are afraid. They stretch in the warm sun. They cuddle by each other.
4. Would you like to be a baby bunny? Why?

Materials:

Yarn, scissors

Preparation:

Cut a string of yarn large enough to encircle all the children. Place it on the rug.

Things to do:

1. The teacher can pretend she is the mother rabbit. The children are the baby bunnies. Use the bunny pattern on page 55 to make bunny headbands for children to wear. Have the baby bunnies stand inside the yarn circle. This is their burrow.
2. The mother bunny can tell her children why it is important to listen. They will need to listen when danger is near. Practice listening. Below are suggestions that the mother bunny can give her children:

- Twitch your nose
- Stomp a foot
- Turn around
- Crouch down and don't move
- Pretend you are asleep
- Sit up on your hind legs
- Move your head side-to-side
- Stop and listen for noises
- Freeze

3. Take turns being the mother or father bunny. This child can think of movements for everyone to follow.

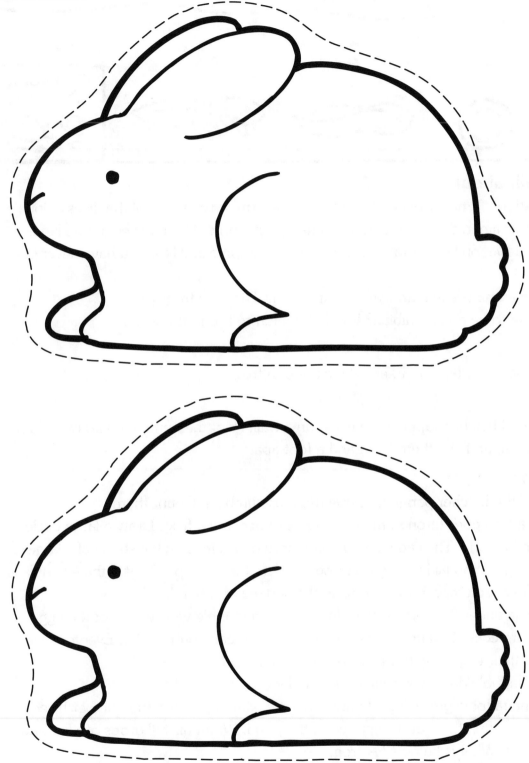

More Ideas:

- Play Freeze Bunny. Place the yarn circle away from the circle time rug. Play the Freeze Dance song. When the teacher sees a bunny wiggle, this bunny leaves the rug and sits in the bunny burrow. Continue to send wiggly bunnies to the burrow. The last bunny standing can call the bunnies out to play.

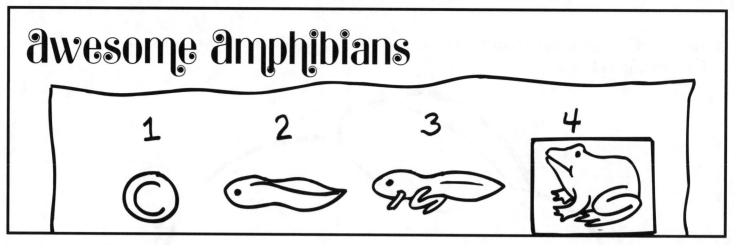

awesome amphibians

Things to talk about:

1. Ask the question: "What is an amphibian?" Brainstorm! It is an animal that lives a double life. It begins its life in the water and then changes its form. Then it lives on the land.
2. Where do you live, on land or in water? Are you an amphibian? No. You have never lived in the water.
3. What are some animals that are called amphibian? They are frogs, newts,
4. Would you like to be an amphibian? Would it be fun to live in the water?

Materials:

Butcher paper, scissors, tape, markers, a picture of a frog

Preparation:

Cut a long sheet of butcher paper. Tape it low on a wall. Print the numbers one, two, three, and four on the paper. Print them large and a foot apart.

Things to do:

1. Sit in front of the butcher paper. Observe the four numbers. Count them.
2. Explain that a frog goes through many changes to become a frog. Draw a large circle under the number one. Then add a black mark, inside the circle, in the shape of a large C. This is a frog egg. Who laid this egg? A frog. Look at the C shape. That is the egg. It lays inside a clump of soft jelly. It then floats to the surface of a pond.
3. Draw a tadpole under the number two. In 10 days, a tadpole wiggles out of the egg. Pretend you are eggs. Curl up on the rug. The teacher can count to 10. Everyone can wiggle out of their egg. Now there are tadpoles in the pond.
4. What does a tadpole do? He swims around and looks for food.
5. Eventually, the tadpole grows legs. Draw a tadpole with legs under the number three. Now he needs to breath air at the surface of the pond. When his tail drops off, he crawls out of the pond. What is he now? A frog.
6. Tape the picture of the frog under the number four. Have everyone clap.

More Ideas:

• Explain that a frog lays many eggs at one time. They are called frog spawn. Have everyone, in turn, draw a circle on the butcher paper, with a C inside. Make sure they are all attached.

The Jump Frog Song

Things to talk about:

1. If a giant frog jumped into our classroom, what would it look like?
2. What did the frog look like when it was born? It was a small black egg, surrounded by a round ball of jelly.
3. Why do you think the egg is inside a soft jelly substance? Does the jelly melt away so the egg can escape? The jelly protects the egg.
4. When you are born, what do you look like?

Materials: None

Preparation: None

Things to do:

Sing the following song to the tune of *Bingo Was His Name-O*. Below are suggested movements:

- For the first verse: Clap the first two lines. For the next three lines, place a fist on the rug and make a jumping motion. Clap the last line.
- For the second verse: Clap the first two lines. For the next three lines, cross your arms over your chest and wiggle back and forth. Clap the last line.
- For the third verse: Clap the first two lines. For the next three lines, make two fists in front of you. When you say the word "tadpole" in each line, pop your first fingers out and wiggle them. Clap the last line.
- For the fourth verse: Clap the first two lines. For the next three lines, clap once on the words, out. When you sing the words, froggy legs, wiggle your fingers. Clap the last line.
- For the fifth verse: Clap the first two lines. For the next three lines, raise a fist in the air on the word, "Now." Keep the fist up for the entire line. Raise it again each time you say the word, "Now." Clap the last line.

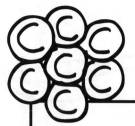  

There was a froggy in a pond,
And Jumpy was his name-O,
Jumpy, jumpy, jumpy frog,
Jumpy, jumpy, jumpy frog,
Jumpy, jumpy, jumpy frog,
And Jumpy was his name-O!

Before he was a little frog,
He was a little egg-O,
Jelly, jelly, jelly egg,
Jelly, jelly, jelly egg,
Jelly, jelly, jelly egg,
And Jumpy was his name-O!

The jelly egg began to wiggle,
Wiggle, wiggle, wiggle-O,
And out came a tadpole,
Out came a tadpole,
Out came a tadpole,
And Jumpy was his name-O!

The tadpole swam around the pond,
And ate and ate and ate-O,
And out popped froggy legs,
Out popped froggy legs,
Out popped froggy legs,
And Jumpy was his name-O!

And then one day, he looked surprised,
And couldn't find his tail-O,
Now I am a jumpy frog,
Now I am a jumpy frog,
Now I am a jumpy frog,
And Jumpy was his name-O!

More Ideas:

• Go to a pet store. Purchase tadpoles and a tank. Take pictures of the different life cycles. Tape them on the table that holds the tank. Cover them with large clear tape. Add pictures of frogs from calendars.

What's New With Newts?

Things to talk about:

1. What is a newt? Brainstorm! It is an amphibian. It lives in the water and also on the land. Has anyone heard the word, salamander? A newt is a type of salamander.
2. If a newt lives in water, where might you find a newt? In your bathtub? In a rain puddle? Newts live in ponds and streams, where they can find food.
3. What kind of food to you think a newt eats? Brainstorm! A newt eats live food. What does that mean? It means small animals that are alive, such as, insects, worms and crickets.
4. How do you eat? You chew with your teeth. How do you think a newt eats? A newt swallows his food whole. He doesn't chew. What does he use his teeth for? He holds his prey with his teeth.

Materials:

A container or jar, paper, scissors, a pen

Preparation:

Cut paper into strips. Make a strip for each child. Print a newt question on each strip, as suggested on page 60.

Things to do:

1. Pretend you are at a pet store. The children are the customers. They want to buy a newt. The teacher is the sales person who works in the store.
2. Each child, in turn, can choose a "pet," question from the jar. The teacher reads the question, and the child answers it.

Suggested questions are:

- What color newt do you want to buy?
- Do you want a young newt or an old newt?
- How big a tank do you want to buy?
- What color gravel do you want for the bottom of your tank?
- How many newts do you want to buy?
- Do you want to buy worms or crickets for your newt to eat?
- What do you want to put in your tank - rocks, plants, gravel?
- How much money can you spend on a tank?
- How much money can you spend on a newt?
- What are you going to name your newt?
- Would you like to buy marbles to drop in your tank? What color marbles?
- Would you like to buy a sales item to go in your tank? We have a pirate ship, a treasure chest, or an alligator.
- You can put a background scene on your tank? Would you like the blue ocean picture or the goldfish picture?
- Do you have a fish net? Would you like to buy one?
- Would you like to buy a book about newts?
- Is there something you would like to ask me about a pet newt?

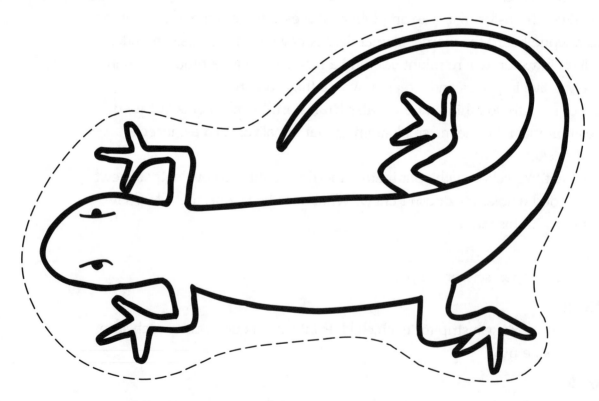

More Ideas:

- Give each child play money. If they answer your question, and buy something from you, they can pay with play money.

 Circle Time—Spring • ©2004 Monday Morning Books, Inc.

The Newt's Song

If you see a newt, Go tell a friend,

Things to talk about:

1. Ask the question: Why would anyone write a song about a newt? Brainstorm! Answers might be: to teach things about the newt, just for fun.
2. If you wrote a song about a newt, what would you put in the song?
3. Can you make up a song about anything? Name things you can sing about.

Materials: None

Preparation: None

Things to do:

1. Sing the following song. As you say the introduction verse, establish a rhythm by clapping on the word "newt" in the first line. Continue to clap slowly throughout the verse with a one...two...one...two rhythm.
2. Sing the remaining song to the tune of *If You're Happy And You Know It*.

- For the first verse:
  Clap all the lines except the sixth one. When you say, "You are just so cute," wiggle a first finger by your face. Do this movement in each verse.
- When you sing the second verse:
  Clap during the verse. When you sing "wave hello," everyone wave.
- When you sing the third verse:
  Clap during the verse. When you sing "a newt," slap both palms of your hands on each cheek.
- When you sing the fourth verse:
  Clap during the verse. When you sing "whoosh," pretend to catch a bug in your fist as it swishes through the air.
- When you sing the fifth verse:
  Clap during the verse. When you sing "I found a newt," raise a fist in the air, twice. Be enthusiastic.

I knew a newt,
I knew a newt,
I knew a newt,
Down by a pond,
And he would say,
And he would say,
Please sing me,
A little newt song!

If you see a little newt,
By a pond,
If you see a little newt,
By a pond,
If you see a little newt,
Say, "You are just so cute!"
If you see a little newt,
By a pond.

If you see a little newt,
Wave hello, (Hello newt!)
If you see a little newt,
Wave hello, (Hello newt!)
If you see a little newt,
Say, "You are just so cute!"
If you see a little newt,
Wave hello, (Hello newt!)

If you see a little newt,
Look surprised, (A newt!)
If you see a little newt,
Look surprised, (A newt!)
If you see a little newt,
Say, "You are just so cute!"
If you see a little newt,
Look surprised, (A newt!)

If you see a little newt,
Catch him a bug, (Whoosh!)
If you see a little newt,
Catch him a bug, (Whoosh!)
If you see a little newt,
Say, "You are just so cute!"
If you see a little newt,
Catch him a bug! (Whoosh!)

If you see a little newt,
Go tell a friend, (I found a newt!)
If you see a little newt,
Go tell a friend, (I found a newt!)
If you see a little newt,
Say, "You are just so cute!"
If you see a little newt,
Go tell a friend, (I found a newt!)

More Ideas:

- Collect pictures of newts from the Internet, calendars, and science books. Make copies when you can. Place the pictures on a poster board or wall. Label the display: What is a newt? Encourage the children to share what they have learned about newts with their parents.

The Earthworm Wiggle

Things to talk about:

1. Ask the question: "What wiggles out of the dirt when it rains?" An earthworm.
2. If an earthworm wiggled onto your arm, what would it feel like? Would it feel dry or wet? Would it feel smooth or rough?
3. Think of words to describe an earthworm. These words might be: brown, round, stretchy, moist, soft, squishy, wiggly, and no legs.
4. How do earthworms move, if they have no legs? They use muscles through their entire body. These muscles push them forward.

Materials:

Brown yarn, scissors, a box

Preparation:

Cut strings of yarn. Make an earthworm for each child. Place the earthworms in a box.

Things to do:

1. Sit in a circle. Pass the box around the circle. Everyone can choose an earthworm.
2. Have everyone hold up their earthworm. Point to the child on your left and say: One little earthworm. Then point to the next child and say: Two little earthworms.
3. Continue to point to each child and say the appropriate number of earthworms.
4. If the last child is number 10, begin the poem with the number 10. Below are suggested movements:

For the first line: Wiggle your worms in front of you.
For the second: Wiggle your worms on the rug.
For the third line: Wiggle them under a fist.
For the fourth line: Bring your fingers and thumb together with one hand.
Wiggle your worm inside the round opening you have made.
For the fifth line: Wiggle your worm from the rug upward.
For the sixth, seventh, eighth, ninth and tenth lines: Swirl them around in the air.
For the eleventh line: After you say boom, drop them to the rug.
For the last line: Slowly move them in an upward direction.

Ten little earthworms wiggling all around,
They wiggled and wiggled under the ground.
They wiggled and wiggled beneath a rock,
They wiggled and wiggled inside an old sock!
They wiggled and squiggled up through the ground,
And twirled and swirled around and around.

Then all of a sudden, it started to rain,
And ten happy earthworms sang and sang,
We love the rain! We love the rain!
But a large clap of thunder, (Boom!)
Scared them down under,
But slowly crept up again!

More Ideas:

• Go to a bait shop. Buy a large cup of earthworms. Place them on a cookie sheet and watch them wiggle.

• Take pictures of the children holding the worms. Catch facial expressions.